WONDER
STARTERS

Homes

Pictures by CHRISTINE SHARR

Published by WONDER BOOKS
A Division of Grosset & Dunlap, Inc.
A NATIONAL GENERAL COMPANY
51 Madison Avenue   New York, N.Y. 10010

About Wonder Starters

Wonder Starters are vocabulary controlled information books for young children. More than ninety per cent of the words in the text will be in the reading vocabulary of the vast majority of young readers. Word and sentence length have also been carefully controlled.

Key new words associated with the topic of each book are repeated with picture explanations in the Starters dictionary at the end. The dictionary can also be used as an index for teaching children to look things up.

Teachers and experts have been consulted on the content and accuracy of the books.

Published in the United States by Wonder Books, a Division of Grosset & Dunlap, Inc., a National General Company.

ISBN: 0-448-09652-8 (Trade Edition)
ISBN: 0-448-06372-7 (Library Edition)

Printed and bound in the United States.

This is our home.
We live at home
with Mommy and Daddy.

1

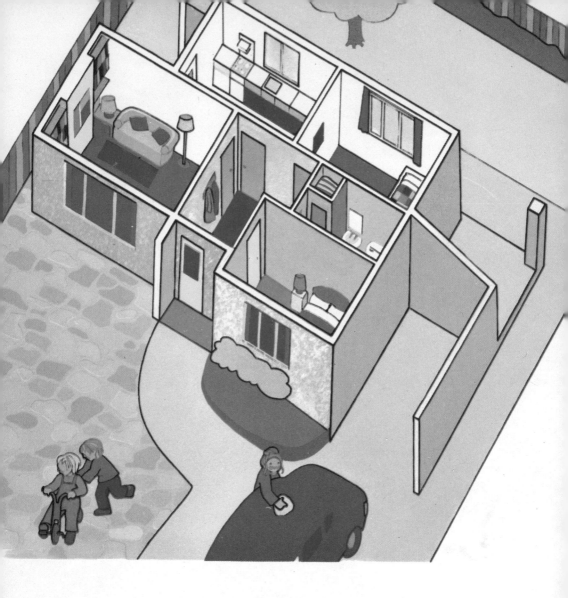

There are five rooms in our home.
Our home is a bungalow.
It has no upstairs.

This is our room.
It has a red carpet.
We have funny pictures on the wall.

This is the kitchen.
Mommy cooks in the kitchen.
She can see out of the window.
4

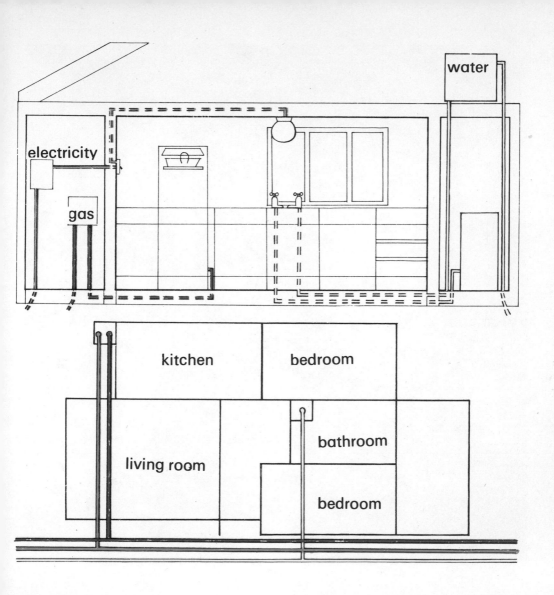

Our kitchen has
electricity, gas and water.

5

Long ago people made homes in caves.
They drew pictures on the wall.
They cooked with fire.

Other people had no caves.
They dug pits for homes.
They put on a roof
to keep them dry.

Some people learned to build.
These people found big stones.
They built stone huts.
8

In cold lands there is snow.
People build huts of snow.
The huts are called igloos.
It is warm inside an igloo.

Here there are lots of trees.
Houses are made of wood.
Thick snow slips off the steep roof.

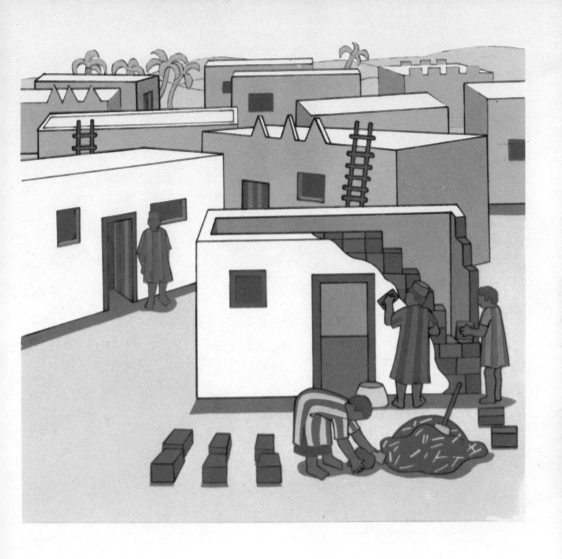

These houses are made of mud.
People make mud bricks.
The sun bakes the mud hard.

These houses are made of bricks, too.
The bricks are small and red.
The bricks are made of baked clay.
12

Gypsies like to move their homes.
Gypsies live in caravans.

13

These people must move their homes.
They take their animals
to find fresh grass.
They live in tents.
14

Other people live in tents, too.
People take tents with them
on camping trips.

15

Kings lived in palaces.
Palaces were very big homes.
Kings were very rich.
16

This is a castle.
Castles were very strong homes.
They were safe in war.

Most homes are near other homes.
These are in a village.
The people can help each other.
They sell things to each other.
18

Lots of homes make a town.
Here is a town of long ago.

19

More and more people live in towns.
They cannot all have houses.
There is no room.
People live in apartment houses.
20